Spotter's Guide to

WILD FLOWERS

of North America

Michael A. Ruggiero
Horticultural Specialist
New York Botanical Garden

Illustrated by Joyce Bee

with additional illustrations
by Will Giles

MAYFLOWER BOOKS
NEW YORK

Contents

Edited and designed by Karen Goaman

Manufactured in Spain by Printer, industria gráfica sa Sant Vicenç dels Horts, Barcelona
D.L. 14.138-1979

Library of Congress Cataloging in Publication Data

Ruggiero, Michael, 1946-
  Spotter's guide to wild flowers of North America.

  Includes index.
  1. Wild flowers – North America – Identification
I. Title.
QK110.R83   582'.13'.097   79-735
ISBN 0-8317-9424-0
ISBN 0-8317-9425-9 pbk.

First American Edition

How to use this book

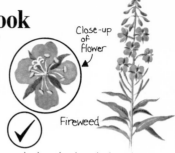

Close-up of Flower

Fireweed

This book will help you to identify some of the wild flowers of the USA and Canada. Take it with you when you go out looking for wild flowers.

The flowers are arranged by color to make it easy for you to look them up. Remember though that some flowers can be any one of two or more colors.

The pictures in circles next to the main illustrations show close-ups of flowers, or a plant's fruits or seeds. These will help you to identify the plant. For example, the picture in the circle beside the illustration of the Fireweed shows a close-up of a single flower.

The description next to each flower will also help you to identify it. The plants are not drawn to scale, but the description gives you the range of their height, measured from the ground. If the plant has a climbing, creeping or trailing stem, the length of its stem is given rather than the height. The description also tells you when the plant flowers. Beside the description is a small blank circle. Each time you see a flower, check it off in the circle.

The names of flowers

Many flowers have more than one common name and may be known by different names in different parts of North America. Only one common name appears in the description of each flower, but some other commonly used names appear in the Index on pages 63-64.

Each plant has a Latin name which remains the same, and this appears in the Index after the common name or names. This is useful to know for further study.

Scorecard

The scorecard on pages 58-62 gives you scores for each flower shown in the book. There are separate scores for different areas of North America: look at the map on page 58 to find out which area you are in.

You can also use the scorecard to find out the areas in which a flower grows, and how common or rare it is in each area: a very common plant scores 5 and a very rare or interesting one scores 25.

What to take

Take this book, plus a notebook and pencils, and a camera, if you have one, so that you can record the flowers you find by drawing or photographing them and making notes. See page 55 for hints on how to do this. Take a tape measure to measure the height of plants and the length of runners. A hand lens will help you to take a closer look at the parts of flower heads (see page 49 for the names of the main parts of a flower).

If you find a flower that is not in this book, your drawing and notes will help you to identify it from other books later. There is a list of useful books on page 57.

Yellow Adder's-tongue ▶
Flowering plant has two leaves mottled with maroon; young plant has one. Usually in large groups in woods. 2-8″ tall. Spring.

Flowers often spotted near base

◀ Yellow Lady's-slipper
Up to six pointed leaves and one or two fragrant flowers. Bogs, marshes and dry to moist woods. 6-28″ tall. From spring to early summer.

Swamp Buttercup ▶
Deeply divided leaves on trailing stems. Look on banks of streams, in woods and meadows. Stems 12-36″ long. From spring to early summer.

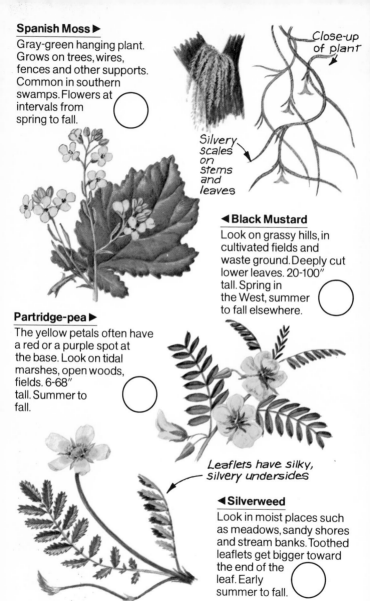

Spanish Moss ▶
Gray-green hanging plant. Grows on trees, wires, fences and other supports. Common in southern swamps. Flowers at intervals from spring to fall.

Close-up of plant

Silvery scales on stems and leaves

◀ Black Mustard
Look on grassy hills, in cultivated fields and waste ground. Deeply cut lower leaves. 20-100" tall. Spring in the West, summer to fall elsewhere.

Partridge-pea ▶
The yellow petals often have a red or a purple spot at the base. Look on tidal marshes, open woods, fields. 6-68" tall. Summer to fall.

Leaflets have silky, silvery undersides

◀ Silverweed
Look in moist places such as meadows, sandy shores and stream banks. Toothed leaflets get bigger toward the end of the leaf. Early summer to fall.

5

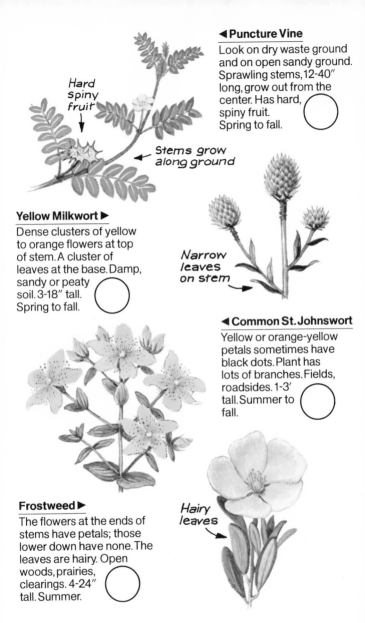

◄ Puncture Vine
Look on dry waste ground and on open sandy ground. Sprawling stems, 12-40" long, grow out from the center. Has hard, spiny fruit. Spring to fall.

Hard spiny fruit →

Stems grow along ground →

Yellow Milkwort ►
Dense clusters of yellow to orange flowers at top of stem. A cluster of leaves at the base. Damp, sandy or peaty soil. 3-18" tall. Spring to fall.

Narrow leaves on stem →

◄ Common St. Johnswort
Yellow or orange-yellow petals sometimes have black dots. Plant has lots of branches. Fields, roadsides. 1-3' tall. Summer to fall.

Frostweed ►
The flowers at the ends of stems have petals; those lower down have none. The leaves are hairy. Open woods, prairies, clearings. 4-24" tall. Summer.

Hairy leaves →

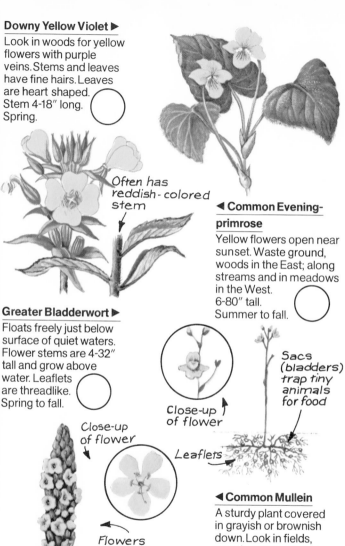

Downy Yellow Violet ▶
Look in woods for yellow flowers with purple veins. Stems and leaves have fine hairs. Leaves are heart shaped. Stem 4-18" long. Spring.

Often has reddish-colored stem

◀ Common Evening-primrose
Yellow flowers open near sunset. Waste ground, woods in the East; along streams and in meadows in the West. 6-80" tall. Summer to fall.

Greater Bladderwort ▶
Floats freely just below surface of quiet waters. Flower stems are 4-32" tall and grow above water. Leaflets are threadlike. Spring to fall.

Close-up of flower

Sacs (bladders) trap tiny animals for food

Close-up of flower

Leaflets

Close-up of flower

Flowers grow in clusters on club shaped head

◀ Common Mullein
A sturdy plant covered in grayish or brownish down. Look in fields, woods, waste ground, or on rocky banks. Up to 6' tall. Spring to fall.

7

Flowers curve downward at tip

◄ Wood-betony
Dense clusters of yellow or red flowers at ends of clustered unbranched stems. 6-16" tall. Look in spring in meadows, woods, prairies and clearings.

Common Monkey-flower ►
Yellow flowers usually spotted red. Leaves are broad and toothed. Stem usually branched. Look in wet places from spring to fall.
Stem 2-40" tall.

Stamens

◄ Yellow Blazing-star
Flowers open toward the evening. Yellow, narrow petals. Lots of stamens. Look in deserts and other sandy places.
8-60" tall.
Summer to fall.

Buffalo-gourd ►
Leaves have an unpleasant smell. Trailing stems are up to 20' long. Gravelly or sandy soil in scrub, grassland, roadsides.
Spring to summer.

Fruit

8

Yellow Sand-verbena ▶

Look in sandy places by the coast. Flowers grow on short stalks in rounded clusters. Sticky, spreading stems 12-40" long. Spring to fall.

Thick leaves on long stalks

Rough, hairy stems and leaves

◀ Black-eyed Susan

Flower heads have dark brown centers and many orange-yellow or yellow petals. Found in fields and woods. 12-40" tall. Spring to summer.

Common Sunflower ▶

Broad, hairy leaves and large flower heads. Grows in fields, waste ground and on roadsides. Summer (spring in West) to fall. 8-13' tall.

◀ Blanket-flower

Petals usually red with yellow tips; sometimes purple, or purple tipped with yellow. Sandy places. 8-24" tall. Late spring to summer.

9

Fruits have parachutes

Tickseed ▶

Yellow flower heads have long stalks. Leaves are narrow. Look in dry gravelly, rocky and/or sandy places. 8-32″ tall. Spring to summer.

◀ Common Dandelion

Plant has a milky sap. Naked flower stalks, each topped by one flower head. Leaves grow in a rosette. Look on open ground. Up to 8″ tall. Spring to fall.

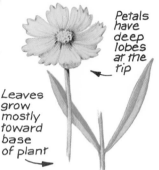

Petals have deep lobes at the tip

Leaves grow mostly toward base of plant

◀ Goldenrod

Look in thickets and in moist open places. Small flower heads are borne in dense clusters. Plant is usually smooth. 20-100″ tall. Summer to fall.

Gumweed ▶

Hairy plant has yellow flower heads. Narrow leaves smell of resin. Look in open places, on wooded hillsides. 4-40″ tall. Spring to summer.

Yellow flower heads

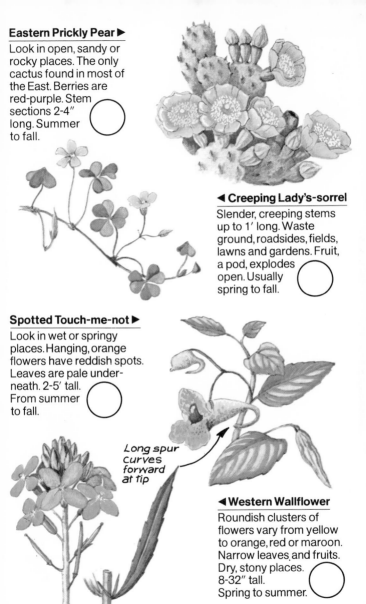

Eastern Prickly Pear ▶
Look in open, sandy or rocky places. The only cactus found in most of the East. Berries are red-purple. Stem sections 2-4″ long. Summer to fall.

◀ Creeping Lady's-sorrel
Slender, creeping stems up to 1′ long. Waste ground, roadsides, fields, lawns and gardens. Fruit, a pod, explodes open. Usually spring to fall.

Spotted Touch-me-not ▶
Look in wet or springy places. Hanging, orange flowers have reddish spots. Leaves are pale underneath. 2-5′ tall. From summer to fall.

Long spur curves forward at tip

◀ Western Wallflower
Roundish clusters of flowers vary from yellow to orange, red or maroon. Narrow leaves and fruits. Dry, stony places. 8-32″ tall. Spring to summer.

11

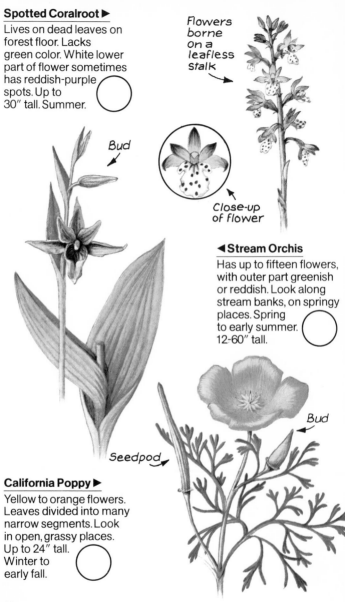

Spotted Coralroot ▶

Lives on dead leaves on forest floor. Lacks green color. White lower part of flower sometimes has reddish-purple spots. Up to 30″ tall. Summer.

Flowers borne on a leafless stalk

Bud

Close-up of flower

◀ Stream Orchis

Has up to fifteen flowers, with outer part greenish or reddish. Look along stream banks, on springy places. Spring to early summer. 12-60″ tall.

Bud

Seedpod

California Poppy ▶

Yellow to orange flowers. Leaves divided into many narrow segments. Look in open, grassy places. Up to 24″ tall. Winter to early fall.

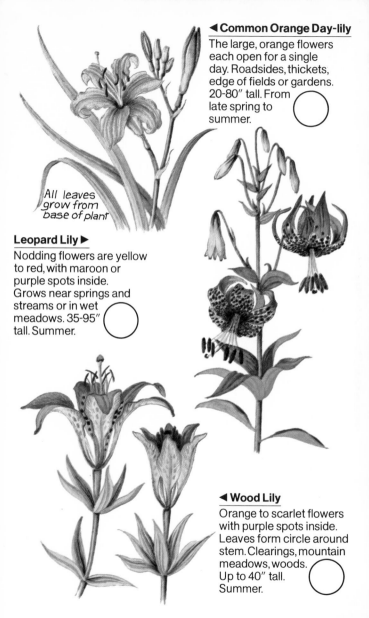

◀ Common Orange Day-lily

The large, orange flowers each open for a single day. Roadsides, thickets, edge of fields or gardens. 20-80" tall. From late spring to summer.

All leaves grow from base of plant

Leopard Lily ▶

Nodding flowers are yellow to red, with maroon or purple spots inside. Grows near springs and streams or in wet meadows. 35-95" tall. Summer.

◀ Wood Lily

Orange to scarlet flowers with purple spots inside. Leaves form circle around stem. Clearings, mountain meadows, woods. Up to 40" tall. Summer.

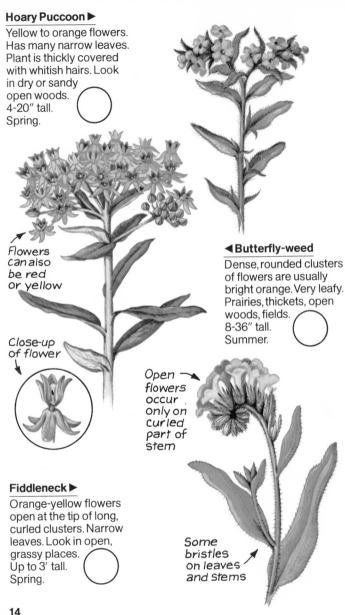

Hoary Puccoon ▶

Yellow to orange flowers.
Has many narrow leaves.
Plant is thickly covered
with whitish hairs. Look
in dry or sandy
open woods.
4-20" tall.
Spring.

*Flowers
can also
be red
or yellow*

*Close-up
of flower*

◀ Butterfly-weed

Dense, rounded clusters
of flowers are usually
bright orange. Very leafy.
Prairies, thickets, open
woods, fields.
8-36" tall.
Summer.

*Open
flowers
occur
only on
curled
part of
stem*

*Some
bristles
on leaves
and stems*

Fiddleneck ▶

Orange-yellow flowers
open at the tip of long,
curled clusters. Narrow
leaves. Look in open,
grassy places.
Up to 3' tall.
Spring.

14

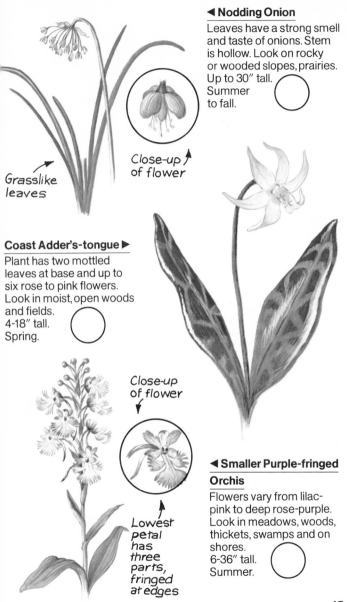

◄ Nodding Onion

Leaves have a strong smell and taste of onions. Stem is hollow. Look on rocky or wooded slopes, prairies. Up to 30″ tall. Summer to fall.

Close-up of flower

Grasslike leaves

Coast Adder's-tongue ►

Plant has two mottled leaves at base and up to six rose to pink flowers. Look in moist, open woods and fields. 4-18″ tall. Spring.

Close-up of flower

Lowest petal has three parts, fringed at edges

◄ Smaller Purple-fringed Orchis

Flowers vary from lilac-pink to deep rose-purple. Look in meadows, woods, thickets, swamps and on shores. 6-36″ tall. Summer.

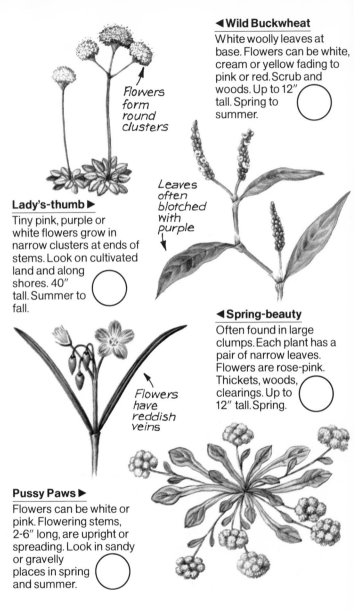

Flowers form round clusters

◄ Wild Buckwheat
White woolly leaves at base. Flowers can be white, cream or yellow fading to pink or red. Scrub and woods. Up to 12" tall. Spring to summer.

Leaves often blotched with purple

Lady's-thumb ►
Tiny pink, purple or white flowers grow in narrow clusters at ends of stems. Look on cultivated land and along shores. 40" tall. Summer to fall.

◄ Spring-beauty
Often found in large clumps. Each plant has a pair of narrow leaves. Flowers are rose-pink. Thickets, woods, clearings. Up to 12" tall. Spring.

Flowers have reddish veins

Pussy Paws ►
Flowers can be white or pink. Flowering stems, 2-6" long, are upright or spreading. Look in sandy or gravelly places in spring and summer.

Bitter Root ▶

Rose-pink or white flower has about fifteen petals. Flowering stem ¾" long. Fleshy leaves at base. Look in rocky mountain places. Spring to summer.

Toothed petal has pale spots near base ↓

Close-up of flower ↑

◀ Deptford Pink

Upright plant with very narrow leaves. Small pink to red flowers. Found in fields and along roadsides. Up to 32" tall. Late spring to summer.

Bouncing Bet ▶

Pink or white flowers. Leaves contain soaplike substance. Found in fields, roadsides, waste ground, railroad banks. 36" tall. Summer to fall.

Leaves end in twining tendrils →

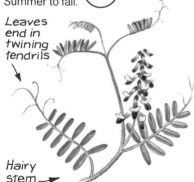

Hairy stem →

◀ Hairy Vetch

Top petal of flower is white, the rest usually violet. Trailing or climbing stems are 20-40" long. Fields and roadsides. From spring to fall.

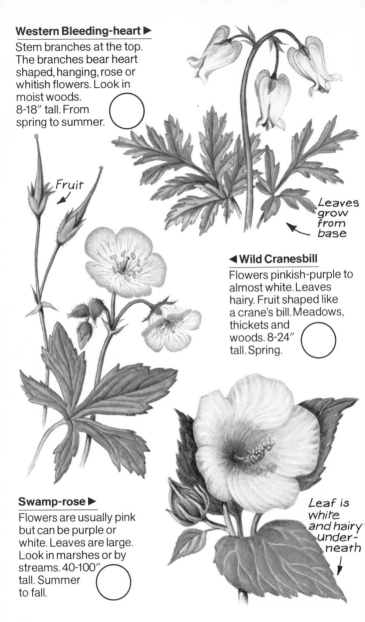

Western Bleeding-heart ▶

Stem branches at the top. The branches bear heart shaped, hanging, rose or whitish flowers. Look in moist woods. 8-18" tall. From spring to summer.

Fruit

Leaves grow from base

◀ Wild Cranesbill

Flowers pinkish-purple to almost white. Leaves hairy. Fruit shaped like a crane's bill. Meadows, thickets and woods. 8-24" tall. Spring.

Swamp-rose ▶

Flowers are usually pink but can be purple or white. Leaves are large. Look in marshes or by streams. 40-100" tall. Summer to fall.

Leaf is white and hairy underneath

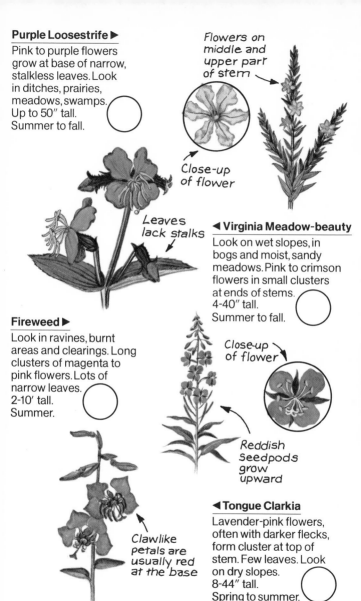

Purple Loosestrife ▶
Pink to purple flowers grow at base of narrow, stalkless leaves. Look in ditches, prairies, meadows, swamps. Up to 50" tall. Summer to fall.

Flowers on middle and upper part of stem →

Close-up of flower

Leaves lack stalks

Fireweed ▶
Look in ravines, burnt areas and clearings. Long clusters of magenta to pink flowers. Lots of narrow leaves. 2-10' tall. Summer.

Clawlike petals are usually red at the base

◀ Virginia Meadow-beauty
Look on wet slopes, in bogs and moist, sandy meadows. Pink to crimson flowers in small clusters at ends of stems. 4-40" tall. Summer to fall.

Close-up of flower ↘

Reddish seedpods grow upward

◀ Tongue Clarkia
Lavender-pink flowers, often with darker flecks, form cluster at top of stem. Few leaves. Look on dry slopes. 8-44" tall. Spring to summer.

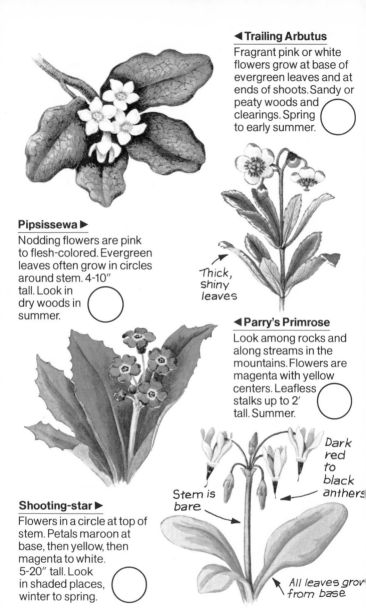

◀ Trailing Arbutus
Fragrant pink or white flowers grow at base of evergreen leaves and at ends of shoots. Sandy or peaty woods and clearings. Spring to early summer.

Pipsissewa ▶
Nodding flowers are pink to flesh-colored. Evergreen leaves often grow in circles around stem. 4-10" tall. Look in dry woods in summer.

Thick, shiny leaves

◀ Parry's Primrose
Look among rocks and along streams in the mountains. Flowers are magenta with yellow centers. Leafless stalks up to 2' tall. Summer.

Dark red to black anthers

Stem is bare

Shooting-star ▶
Flowers in a circle at top of stem. Petals maroon at base, then yellow, then magenta to white. 5-20" tall. Look in shaded places, winter to spring.

All leaves grow from base

Rose-pink ▶

Fragrant flowers have pink petals, yellow centers. Leaves are stalkless. Look in clearings, open woods, prairies. 8-36" tall. Summer to fall.

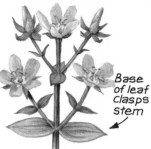

Base of leaf clasps stem

Leaves borne in opposite pairs

◀ Spreading Dogbane

Plant produces a milky juice when broken. Many branches. Grows on dry soil at edges of woods and in thickets. 4-20" tall. Summer.

Gilia ▶

Stem branches form rounded flower clusters. Most leaves are at base of plant. Look in dry places in scrub. 4-12" tall. Spring.

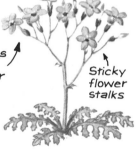

Flowers can be violet or white

Sticky flower stalks

◀ Rose Vervain

Flowers are usually pink, rose or magenta. Look in sandy or rocky places, fields and on roadsides. Branches are 4-16" long. Spring to fall.

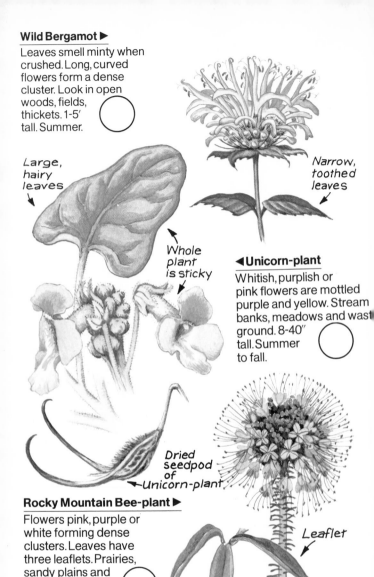

Wild Bergamot ▶

Leaves smell minty when crushed. Long, curved flowers form a dense cluster. Look in open woods, fields, thickets. 1-5' tall. Summer.

Large, hairy leaves

Narrow, toothed leaves

Whole plant is sticky

◀ Unicorn-plant

Whitish, purplish or pink flowers are mottled purple and yellow. Stream banks, meadows and waste ground. 8-40" tall. Summer to fall.

Dried seedpod of Unicorn-plant

Rocky Mountain Bee-plant ▶

Flowers pink, purple or white forming dense clusters. Leaves have three leaflets. Prairies, sandy plains and waste ground. 1-3' tall. Summer.

Leaflet

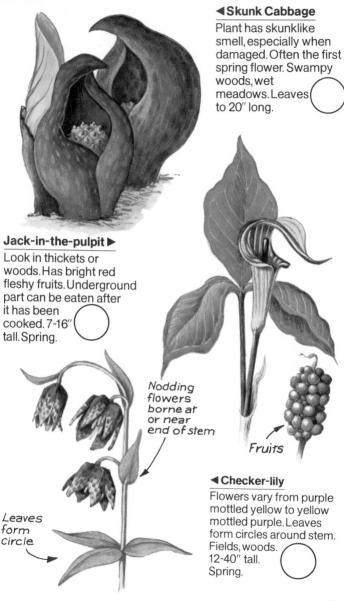

◄ Skunk Cabbage
Plant has skunklike smell, especially when damaged. Often the first spring flower. Swampy woods, wet meadows. Leaves to 20″ long.

Jack-in-the-pulpit ►
Look in thickets or woods. Has bright red fleshy fruits. Underground part can be eaten after it has been cooked. 7-16″ tall. Spring.

Nodding flowers borne at or near end of stem

Leaves form circle

Fruits

◄ Checker-lily
Flowers vary from purple mottled yellow to yellow mottled purple. Leaves form circles around stem. Fields, woods. 12-40″ tall. Spring.

23

Wild Ginger ▶

A creeping plant that grows in groups. Bell shaped flower grows near ground between a pair of leaves. Moist woods, shady ledges. Spring.

Heart or kidney shaped leaves

Plant smells of ginger when broken

Petals have long, curved spurs

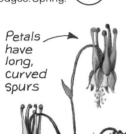

◀ Wild Columbine

Leaves are divided into many segments and grow on long stalks. Flowers are usually red. Look in rocky woods. To 20" tall. Spring to early summer.

Narrow leaves

Red Maids ▶

Flowers are rose-red to red-purple (or, rarely, white). Look in grassy places and cultivated fields. Branches 4-16" long. Winter to spring.

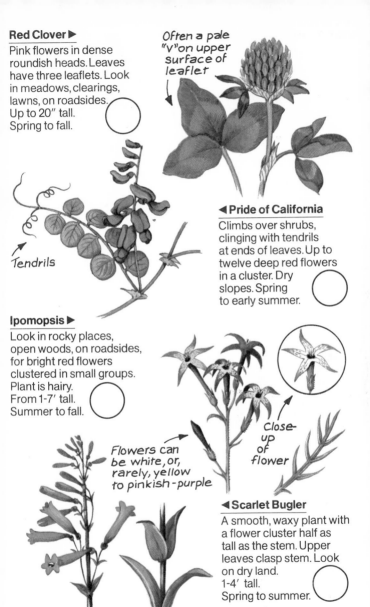

Red Clover ▶

Pink flowers in dense roundish heads. Leaves have three leaflets. Look in meadows, clearings, lawns, on roadsides. Up to 20" tall. Spring to fall.

Often a pale "V" on upper surface of leaflet

Tendrils

◀ Pride of California

Climbs over shrubs, clinging with tendrils at ends of leaves. Up to twelve deep red flowers in a cluster. Dry slopes. Spring to early summer.

Ipomopsis ▶

Look in rocky places, open woods, on roadsides, for bright red flowers clustered in small groups. Plant is hairy. From 1-7' tall. Summer to fall.

Close-up of flower

Flowers can be white, or, rarely, yellow to pinkish-purple

◀ Scarlet Bugler

A smooth, waxy plant with a flower cluster half as tall as the stem. Upper leaves clasp stem. Look on dry land. 1-4' tall. Spring to summer.

Indian Warrior ▶

Flowers borne in clusters
on the end of the stem.
Deeply divided leaves.
Look on dry slopes, scrub,
woodland, pine
woods. 4-20" tall.
Winter to summer.

◀ Scarlet Paintbrush

Upright plant with few
stems. Narrow leaves.
Look in moist, shady
places in mountains.
From 16-32" tall.
Spring
to fall.

*A sticky,
hairy
plant*

Seaside Petunia ▶

Purple or reddish-
violet flowers with
white or yellow tubes.
Look on beaches, dried
pool and stream
beds. 4-16" tall.
Spring to fall.

Cardinal-flower ▶
Bright red flowers. Many narrow leaves on an unbranched stem 1-6′ tall. Look on damp shores, in meadows and swamps. Summer through to fall.

Leaves are irregularly toothed

Leaves are downy underneath

◀ Ironweed
Narrow, toothed leaves and many bell-shaped heads of tubular, purple flowers. Look in moist woods in summer through to fall. 3-10′ tall.

Purple Blazing-star ▶
Many stems and smooth, narrow leaves. Stems bear dense clusters of purple flowers. Dry prairies and plains, late summer to fall. 6-32″ tall.

Base of flower head

Very narrow leaves

◀ Bull Thistle
Main leaves and small leaves below purple flower heads are prickly. Look in pastures, clearings and on roadsides. 20-80″ tall. Summer to fall.

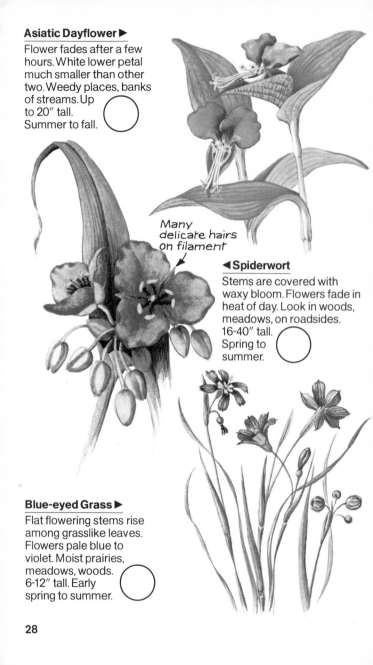

Asiatic Dayflower ▶

Flower fades after a few hours. White lower petal much smaller than other two. Weedy places, banks of streams. Up to 20″ tall. Summer to fall.

Many delicate hairs on filament

◀ Spiderwort

Stems are covered with waxy bloom. Flowers fade in heat of day. Look in woods, meadows, on roadsides. 16-40″ tall. Spring to summer.

Blue-eyed Grass ▶

Flat flowering stems rise among grasslike leaves. Flowers pale blue to violet. Moist prairies, meadows, woods. 6-12″ tall. Early spring to summer.

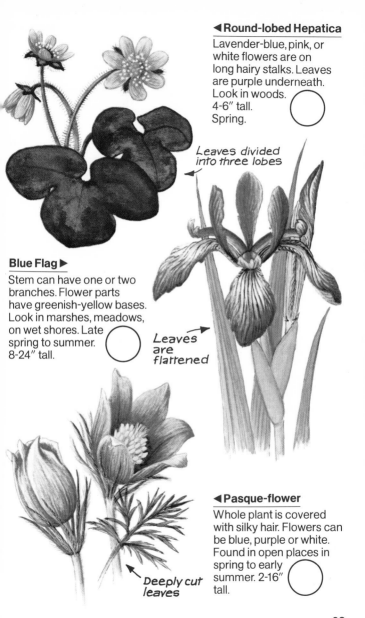

◀ Round-lobed Hepatica
Lavender-blue, pink, or white flowers are on long hairy stalks. Leaves are purple underneath. Look in woods. 4-6″ tall. Spring.

Leaves divided into three lobes

Blue Flag ▶
Stem can have one or two branches. Flower parts have greenish-yellow bases. Look in marshes, meadows, on wet shores. Late spring to summer. 8-24″ tall.

Leaves are flattened

◀ Pasque-flower
Whole plant is covered with silky hair. Flowers can be blue, purple or white. Found in open places in spring to early summer. 2-16″ tall.

Deeply cut leaves

29

Blue Columbine ▶

Bright blue sepals and white petals. Leaves at base are divided into roundish segments. Grows high in the mountains. 8-32" tall. Summer.

Spur (sepals forming tube)

◀ Larkspur

Flowers grow in loose clusters. Color can be blue or violet; sometimes marked with white. Look in woods and on prairies. 4-36" tall. Spring.

Leaflets attached at same point

Lupine ▶

Hairy plant with upright, slender stem. Flowers from light blue to lilac. Look in open fields and on slopes in the spring. 8-16" tall.

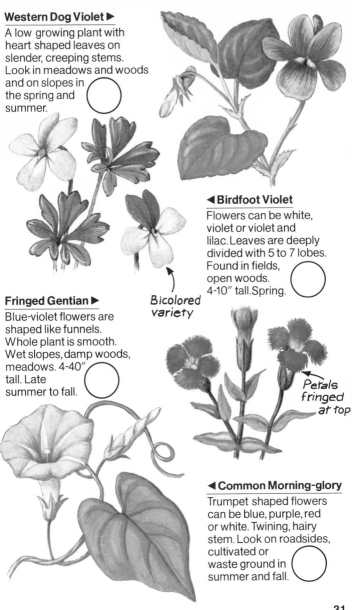

Western Dog Violet ▶

A low growing plant with heart shaped leaves on slender, creeping stems. Look in meadows and woods and on slopes in the spring and summer.

◀ Birdfoot Violet

Flowers can be white, violet or violet and lilac. Leaves are deeply divided with 5 to 7 lobes. Found in fields, open woods. 4-10" tall. Spring.

Fringed Gentian ▶

Blue-violet flowers are shaped like funnels. Whole plant is smooth. Wet slopes, damp woods, meadows. 4-40" tall. Late summer to fall.

Bicolored variety

Petals fringed at top

◀ Common Morning-glory

Trumpet shaped flowers can be blue, purple, red or white. Twining, hairy stem. Look on roadsides, cultivated or waste ground in summer and fall.

Wild Heliotrope ▶

Blue to purplish-blue or cream flowers. Stems can stand upright, lean or lie flat. Slopes, dunes, fields. Stems up to 50" long. Spring to summer.

Stem is bristly

◀ Blue Phlox

Blue to purple flowers in an open rounded cluster on stems 4-20" tall. Has few leaves. Look on rocky slopes or in woods. Spring.

Flowers can be white with black dots on petals

Baby Blue-eyes ▶

Flowers are usually bright blue with a light center. Look on slopes in grassland and scrub. Stems 4-12" long. Winter to early summer.

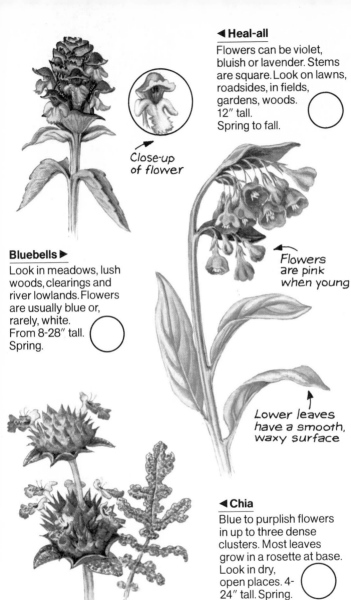

◀ Heal-all

Flowers can be violet, bluish or lavender. Stems are square. Look on lawns, roadsides, in fields, gardens, woods. 12" tall. Spring to fall.

Close-up of flower

Bluebells ▶

Look in meadows, lush woods, clearings and river lowlands. Flowers are usually blue or, rarely, white. From 8-28" tall. Spring.

Flowers are pink when young

Lower leaves have a smooth, waxy surface

◀ Chia

Blue to purplish flowers in up to three dense clusters. Most leaves grow in a rosette at base. Look in dry, open places. 4-24" tall. Spring.

◀ Horse-nettle
A prickly, hairy plant.
Pale violet to white
star shaped flowers.
Look in fields, waste
ground, woods.
12-40" tall.
Spring to fall.

Spines on
underside
of leaf

Spur

Close-up
of flower

Old-field Toadflax ▶
Loose clusters of violet,
spurred flowers. Narrow
leaves. A very slender
plant. Found in sandy
places. 32"
tall. Spring
to fall.

Close-up
of flower

◀ American Brooklime
A smooth, fleshy plant
with toothed leaves.
Violet or lilac flowers.
Look near shallow water,
swamps, streams.
Up to 40" long.
Summer.

Monkey-flower ▶
Blue to pinkish flowers
borne between upper leaves
and stem. Look in meadows,
near shores and other
wet places. 1-4'
tall. Summer
to fall.

34

Snapdragon ▶

A sticky, hairy plant with broad leaves and loose clusters of violet flowers. Look in dry, used places in scrub. 4-16" tall. Spring to summer.

Flowers in circle around stem ↘

Plant can be upright or spreading

◀ Chinese Houses

Flower's upper lip is white or lilac. Lower one is rose-purple or violet. Look in shady places and on dry slopes. 8-20" tall. Spring to summer.

One-flowered Cancer-root ▶

Grows and feeds on roots of other plants. Two or three flowers in West, one elsewhere. Damp woods, thickets. 1-10" tall. Spring to early summer.

Flowers can be pale lavender, lilac or white ↗

◀ Hairy Ruellia

Almost stalkless flowers, violet to lavender, borne between upper leaves and stem. Look on prairies, in clearings, woods. 1-2' tall. Summer.

35

◀ Bluets

Blue to lilac flowers with yellow centers. Rosette of leaves at base of stem. Look in meadows, woods and fields. 2-8" tall. Spring to summer.

Wild Teasel ▶

Plant has prickly stem. Leaves are often prickly at the edges. Tiny violet flowers. Waste ground and roadsides. 20-80" tall. Summer to fall.

◀ Venus' Looking-glass

Look on roadsides, fields and gardens for bluish-white to bluish-violet flowers. Leaves alternate on stem. 1-2' tall. Spring to summer.

Flowers rarely white

Broad leaves clasp the stem

Bell shaped flowers can be purplish-blue or violet-blue

Harebell ▶

A slender plant, often with lots of branches. Shape of leaf varies. Look on banks, ledges, in meadows, woods. 4-20" tall. Summer to fall.

Prairie Flax ▶
Plant has very narrow leaves and leafy clusters of blue flowers. Usually has several stems. Banks, prairies, forests. 6-30" tall. Spring to fall.

New England Aster ◀
Flower heads have yellow centers and purple to pink petals. Look in fields, meadows, thickets, along roadsides. 12-40" tall. Summer to fall.

Common Chicory ▶
Flower heads are usually blue but they can be pink or white. Look on waste ground, in fields and on roadsides. 12-40" tall. Spring to fall.

Leaves lobed or toothed

Air filled base of leaf acts as a float

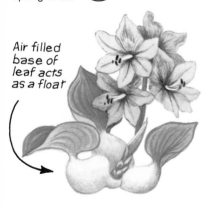

Water-hyacinth ◀
A floating plant common in ponds, streams and ditches. Showy flowers on stalks 4-16" tall. Chokes waterways in the south. Spring to summer.

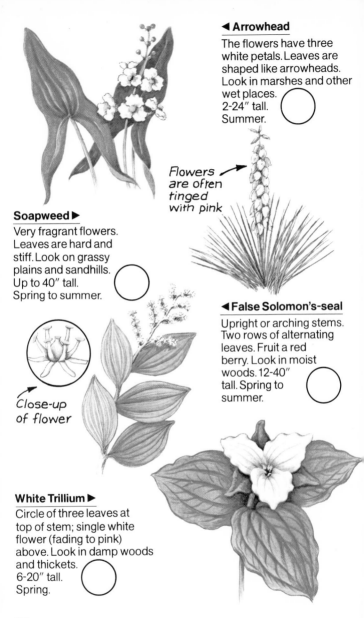

◀ Arrowhead
The flowers have three white petals. Leaves are shaped like arrowheads. Look in marshes and other wet places.
2-24" tall.
Summer.

Flowers are often tinged with pink

Soapweed ▶
Very fragrant flowers. Leaves are hard and stiff. Look on grassy plains and sandhills. Up to 40" tall. Spring to summer.

Close-up of flower

◀ False Solomon's-seal
Upright or arching stems. Two rows of alternating leaves. Fruit a red berry. Look in moist woods. 12-40" tall. Spring to summer.

White Trillium ▶
Circle of three leaves at top of stem; single white flower (fading to pink) above. Look in damp woods and thickets.
6-20" tall.
Spring.

False Hellebore ▶

Greenish-white flowers grow in branching clusters. Look in wet places and in mountain fields. 3-6' tall. Summer.

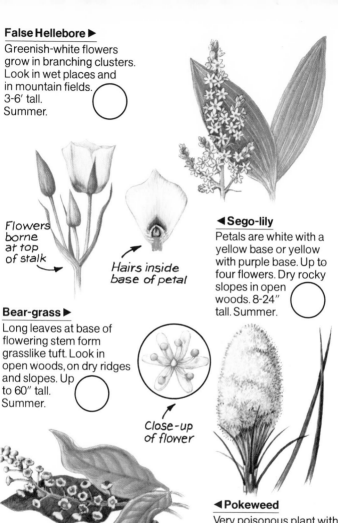

Flowers borne at top of stalk

Hairs inside base of petal

◀ Sego-lily

Petals are white with a yellow base or yellow with purple base. Up to four flowers. Dry rocky slopes in open woods. 8-24" tall. Summer.

Bear-grass ▶

Long leaves at base of flowering stem form grasslike tuft. Look in open woods, on dry ridges and slopes. Up to 60" tall. Summer.

Close-up of flower

◀ Pokeweed

Very poisonous plant with unpleasant smell. Small flowers white to pink. Look in clearings and on roadsides. Up to 10' tall. Summer to fall.

39

◄ Miner's Lettuce
Found mainly in moist, shady places. Was eaten as a salad by American Indians miners and settlers. 12" tall. Winter, spring to summer. ◯

Stems grow through center of leaf

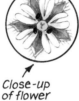

Common Chickweed ►
Look on cultivated ground, waste ground, in woods and thickets. Small white flowers. Trailing stems up to 32" long. From spring to fall. ◯

Close-up of flower

◄ Anemone
Found in woods and on prairies. Leaves on stems have no stalks and grow in a circle around stem. One to six flowers. 8-28" tall. Spring to early summer. ◯

Nodding flowers

Sepals

Early Meadow-rue ►
Plant has drooping flowers and leaves. Four or five sepals vary from greenish-white to purplish-brown. Moist woods. 8-30" tall. Spring. ◯

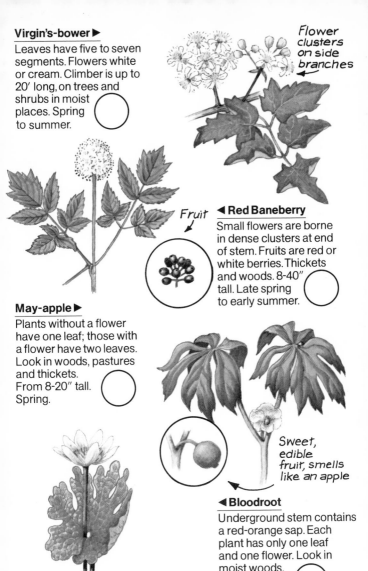

Virgin's-bower ▶

Leaves have five to seven segments. Flowers white or cream. Climber is up to 20′ long, on trees and shrubs in moist places. Spring to summer.

Flower clusters on side branches

◀ Red Baneberry

Fruit

Small flowers are borne in dense clusters at end of stem. Fruits are red or white berries. Thickets and woods. 8-40″ tall. Late spring to early summer.

May-apple ▶

Plants without a flower have one leaf; those with a flower have two leaves. Look in woods, pastures and thickets. From 8-20″ tall. Spring.

Sweet, edible fruit, smells like an apple

◀ Bloodroot

Underground stem contains a red-orange sap. Each plant has only one leaf and one flower. Look in moist woods. 6″ tall. Spring.

Prickly Poppy ▶

Has fleshy leaves. Sap
is bright yellow. Look in
waste ground, on prairies,
hills and roadsides.
16-32" tall.
Spring to
early fall.

◀ Dutchman's-breeches

Between four and ten
hanging flowers, usually
white with cream tips.
Finely divided leaves.
Look in woods.
8-12" tall.
Spring.

*Leaves
grow from
base of plant*

Grass-of-Parnassus ▶

White petals have green
or yellow veins. Each
stalk bears one flower.
Leaves grow from base.
Wet meadows and
bogs. 4-24" tall.
Summer to fall.

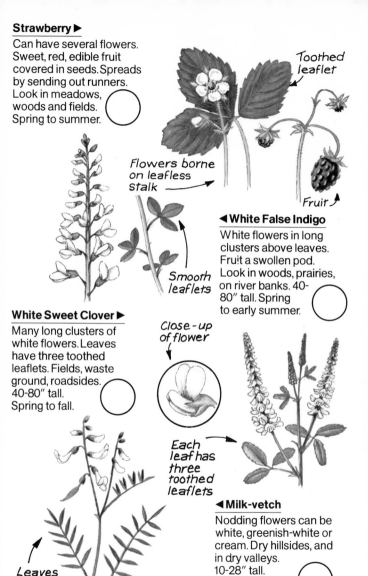

Strawberry ▶
Can have several flowers. Sweet, red, edible fruit covered in seeds. Spreads by sending out runners. Look in meadows, woods and fields. Spring to summer.

Toothed leaflet

Flowers borne on leafless stalk

Fruit

Smooth leaflets

◀ White False Indigo
White flowers in long clusters above leaves. Fruit a swollen pod. Look in woods, prairies, on river banks. 40-80" tall. Spring to early summer.

White Sweet Clover ▶
Many long clusters of white flowers. Leaves have three toothed leaflets. Fields, waste ground, roadsides. 40-80" tall. Spring to fall.

Close-up of flower

Each leaf has three toothed leaflets

◀ Milk-vetch
Nodding flowers can be white, greenish-white or cream. Dry hillsides, and in dry valleys. 10-28" tall. Spring to early summer.

Leaves have narrow leaflets

43

A circle of leaves grows where stem branches →

◄ Flowering Spurge

Look in woods, prairies, fields and on roadsides. Leaves and stems contain milky juice. Flowers in rounded clusters. Up to 40″ tall. Late spring to fall.

Tufted Evening-primrose ►

Plant stemless or with a short stem. Narrow leaves. White flowers fading to pink; open near sunset. Dry, rocky slopes. 4-10″ tall. Spring to fall.

◄ Wild Carrot

Clusters of flowers all white except for pink or purple one at center. Waste ground, fields and roadsides. 1-4′ tall. Spring to fall.

Cow-parsnip ►

Many tiny white flowers in big rounded clusters. Ribbed, hollow stem. Large leaves. Moist places, roadsides. 3-10′ tall. Spring to summer.

Bunchberry ▶

Tiny greenish-white to creamy-yellow flowers form a cluster which looks like a single flower. Moist woods, thickets. 2-12" tall. Spring to summer.

White petallike leaves

Flowers in center

Red berries

Scalelike leaves

◀ Indian-pipe

Whole plant is white to pinkish with no green color. Fleshy stem with nodding flower. Feeds on decaying matter in woods. 2-12" tall. Spring to fall.

Shinleaf ▶

Leaves are evergreen and cluster near the ground. Nodding, fragrant flowers are white to cream. Look in dry to moist woods. 5-12" tall. Summer.

Stalk can bear three to twelve flowers

Flowering Stalk is leafless

Petals have purple streaks or dots

◀ Monument Plant

A stout plant with many leaves at base and circles of narrow ones on stem. Flowers in big clusters. Open pine woods. 3-7' tall. Summer.

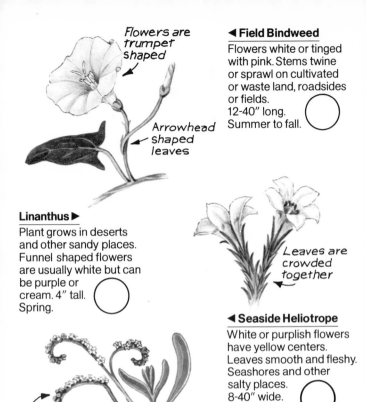

Flowers are trumpet shaped

Arrowhead shaped leaves

◄ Field Bindweed
Flowers white or tinged with pink. Stems twine or sprawl on cultivated or waste land, roadsides or fields.
12-40" long.
Summer to fall.

Linanthus ►
Plant grows in deserts and other sandy places. Funnel shaped flowers are usually white but can be purple or cream. 4" tall. Spring.

Leaves are crowded together

◄ Seaside Heliotrope
White or purplish flowers have yellow centers. Leaves smooth and fleshy. Seashores and other salty places.
8-40" wide.
Spring to fall.

Flowers grow in clusters on one side of stem

Jimsonweed ►
Very poisonous. White or pale violet flowers grow where stem branches. Cultivated or waste ground. Up to 5' tall. Spring (in South) to fall.

Beardtongue ▶

Flowers are white or white tinted with purple. Leaves smooth with sharp points. Look in meadows, open woods. Up to 5' tall. Spring to summer.

Flowers are bearded inside

Fruit

◀ Partridgeberry

Trailing stems form mats. Flowers borne in pairs. Evergreen leaves can have white parts. Fruit a red, edible berry. Slightly raised ground in woods. Summer.

Yerba Mansa ▶

Spikes of tiny petalless flowers with petallike leaves at base. Looks like one flower. Stream edges, wet flats, meadows. 4-20" tall. Spring to fall.

Flowers

Most leaves are at base of plant

◀ Thoroughwort

Many heads of whitish flowers in flattened clusters. Look on wet shores, in thickets and low woods. 1-5' tall. Summer to fall.

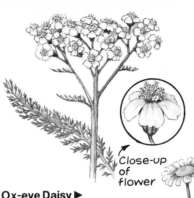

Close-up
of
flower

◄ Common Yarrow

Small flower heads in dense clusters. White to pinkish petals. Roadsides, fields, or in West, woods and scrub. 4-40" tall. Summer to fall.

Ox-eye Daisy ►

Flower heads have yellow centers and many white petals. Look in fields, waste ground, on roadsides. 8-40" tall. Late spring to fall.

Petals can be lavender

Stem leaves are clasping

◄ Common Fleabane

Narrow, stalkless leaves. Pink to white petals with yellow centers. Banks of streams, moist thickets, shores. 4-40" tall. Spring to summer.

Fragrant Water-lily ►

Fragrant flower opens in the morning. Circular, floating leaves about 10" in diameter. Look in ponds, lakes and ditches. Summer.

Parts of a plant

When you find a wild flower, look closely at the flower head and the leaves; this will help you to identify it. These pictures show some of the different parts of a flower, different leaf shapes and the arrangements of the leaves on the stem.

Flowers

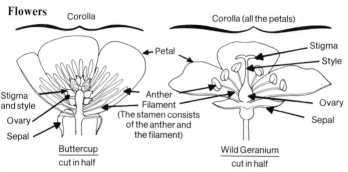

Buttercup cut in half

Wild Geranium cut in half

The stigma, style and ovary are the female parts of the flower, and the stamens are the male parts.

Pollen from the stamens is received by the stigma. It causes seeds to grow inside the ovary.

Leaves

There are many different leaf shapes; leaves can also be arranged in different ways on the stem.

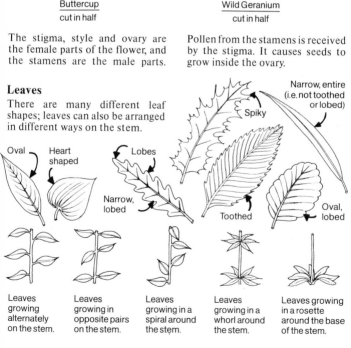

Leaves growing alternately on the stem.

Leaves growing in opposite pairs on the stem.

Leaves growing in a spiral around the stem.

Leaves growing in a whorl around the stem.

Leaves growing in a rosette around the base of the stem.

How seeds are formed

All plants produce seeds to form new plants. Pollen from the male part of the flower (the anthers) must first be received by the female part (the stigma). This process is called pollination. Pollen is the yellow powder which sticks to your fingers when you touch the center of a flower.

Pollen is usually carried from one flower to another of the same kind by insects or by wind. After pollination, the male cells from the pollen fuse (join) with the female "egg" cells in the ovary. The petals wither, the ovary swells and a fruit forms; seeds form inside the ovary.

Insect-pollinated flowers

Insects are attracted to these flowers by their bright color, scent and sometimes by a sweet liquid called nectar produced at the base of the petals. An insect lands on a flower and pollen sticks to its body; when it visits another flower of the same kind, pollen may rub off on to the stigma.

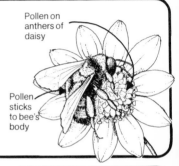

Pollen on anthers of daisy

Pollen sticks to bee's body

Wind-pollinated flowers

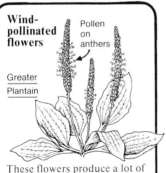

Pollen on anthers

Greater Plantain

These flowers produce a lot of light pollen which is carried by the wind to other flowers of the same kind. They do not need to attract insects, and are not brightly colored or scented and do not produce nectar.

Flower to fruit: Strawberry

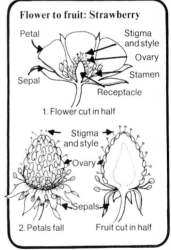

Petal

Stigma and style

Ovary

Sepal

Stamen

Receptacle

1. Flower cut in half

Stigma and style

Ovary

Sepals

2. Petals fall   Fruit cut in half

How seeds are spread

The seeds inside the fruit must now be released so that the following year they will take root and begin to grow. They must also find new places to grow in. The seeds are scattered in many different ways (see the pictures below). Look at the fruits you find on wild flowers and try to figure out how they spread their seeds.

Seeds may stay alive for months or years until the right balance of water, warmth and air makes them grow. Then a shoot will grow up from the seed and a root will grow down into the soil. The plant will then flower and the whole process will begin again.

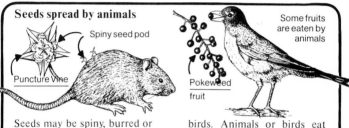

Seeds spread by animals

Spiny seed pod

Puncture Vine

Some fruits are eaten by animals

Pokeweed fruit

Seeds may be spiny, burred or hooked so they catch on to the coats of animals or feathers of birds. Animals or birds eat some fruits and the seeds pass through their bodies.

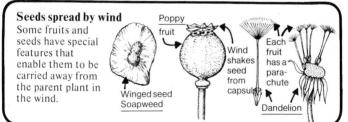

Seeds spread by wind

Some fruits and seeds have special features that enable them to be carried away from the parent plant in the wind.

Poppy fruit

Winged seed Soapweed

Wind shakes seed from capsule

Each fruit has a parachute

Dandelion

Seeds spread by explosion

Some plants form pods which explode or twist open, scattering seeds away from plant.

Creeping Lady's-sorrel

Seeds spread by water

Some fruits and seeds can float in water and may be carried away in the water current.

Water-lily fruit

Where to look

Here are some of the places where you could look for wild flowers, and the sort of flowers you may find in them.

Towns: You may see flowers growing in the cracks of sidewalks and walls, as well as in vacant lots, railroad yards, parking lots and gardens. Their seeds are usually spread by wind. They must be tough to live in the poor soils and dirty air.

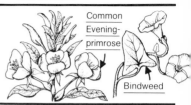

Common Evening-primrose

Bindweed

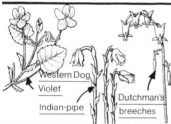

Western Dog Violet

Indian-pipe

Dutchman's breeches

Forests: The best time to look for flowers in forests is in spring, before the leaves of the trees start to grow and keep the sunlight from reaching the forest floor. Most plants need light to grow. One species which can live in the dim light of the summer forest is the Indian Pipe, which feeds on dead leaves.

Seashore: The plants you will find on the shore must survive strong winds, harsh sunlight, salt spray and lack of fresh water. Like desert plants, many have long roots to search out water deep in the sand; their long roots and fleshy leaves also help them to grip the mud, sand or stones and keep them from blowing over.

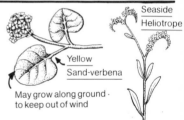

Seaside Heliotrope

Yellow Sand-verbena

May grow along ground to keep out of wind

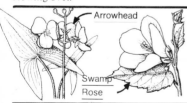

Arrowhead

Swamp Rose

Marshes and swamps: Many wetland plants have thick, tangled root systems that trap mud; this gives them a firmer base from which to grow and helps to raise them above water. But be careful when you are looking here, and stay on paths.

Fields and roadsides: Look on the edges of fields where crops are grown. The plants you will find on roadsides are hardy and can survive the exhaust fumes of cars.

Prairies and plains: Wild flowers growing here must be hardy enough to survive summer droughts and strong winds; they help protect the soil if the grasses wither.

How plants adapt

Plants grow in many places – including water, on mountains and even the desert. Here are some of the ways in which flowering plants have adapted, enabling them to grow in these places.

Deserts

The wild flowers you find in the desert show how well plants can adapt to difficult conditions.

Plants lose water through their leaves, so many desert plants have small leaves to help prevent this. Many of course shed their leaves quite regularly during dry seasons.

Notice that desert plants are often widely, and evenly, spaced; this is to give each plant a large area from which to draw water. Many plants have long roots to search out water deep in the ground.

The seeds of desert plants are very tough and able to remain alive without growing for years. As soon as the rainfall has been heavy enough, they sprout and flower. Some plants will complete their life cycle, that is flower and produce fruit, in a very short time to take advantage of more moist conditions.

Cacti are especially well adapted to life in the desert. They can store water inside their thick, fleshy stems. Their spines protect them from being eaten by thirsty animals. They have no leaves, so no water is lost in this way.

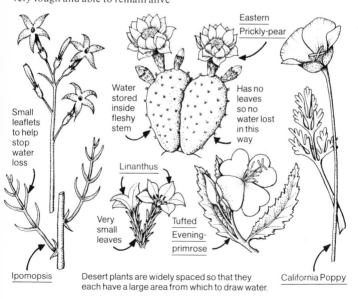

Eastern
Prickly-pear

Water stored inside fleshy stem

Has no leaves so no water lost in this way

Small leaflets to help stop water loss

Linanthus

Very small leaves

Tufted Evening-primrose

Ipomopsis

Desert plants are widely spaced so that they each have a large area from which to draw water.

California Poppy

How plants adapt

Mountains

Although they look delicate, wild flowers growing in the mountains are some of the hardiest of plants.

Many grow in low thick mats, hugging the ground to keep out of the wind and to trap warmer air from the soil. Some have hairy stems to help trap heat. Many also contain a chemical in their fluid which stops them freezing.

Some plants will seem to flower all spring and summer: they begin to bloom on the lower slopes in the spring, and may then flower higher and higher up the mountain as summer comes and the snow melts.

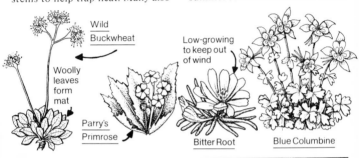

Wild
Buckwheat

Woolly
leaves
form
mat

Low-growing
to keep out
of wind

Parry's
Primrose

Bitter Root

Blue Columbine

Rivers, Streams, Ponds and Lakes

Look on the banks and in the water itself for wild flowers. Plants growing in the water may be rooted to the bottom, like the Water-lily, or float freely, like Bladderwort.

The Water-lily leaf, or pad, is well adapted to water life; it has air sacs inside to help keep it afloat.

The top surface of the pad is waxy and water runs off it.

Only the flowering stem of the Bladderwort shows above the water. Its floating "leaves" have small sacs called bladders, which trap tiny animals in the water for food.

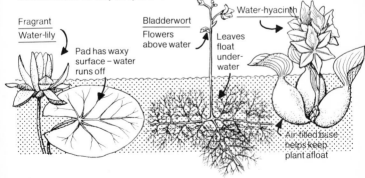

Fragrant
Water-lily

Pad has waxy
surface – water
runs off

Bladderwort
Flowers
above water

Leaves
float
under-
water

Water-hyacinth

Air-filled base
helps keep
plant afloat

Flower record book

Keep a record of all the wild flowers you find. If you use a loose-leaf binder you can add pages whenever you wish.

Take a full page for each flower you find. Draw or paint the plant, including its stem and leaves; make notes beside the picture of where and when you found the flower, its height and any other interesting points you notice.

If you are certain that a flower is a very common and widespread one, and as long as you do not find it in a park where collecting is not permitted, you can pick it and press it. Put the flower between two sheets of blotting paper and rest some heavy books on top. When the flower is dry, put a bit of glue on the stem and carefully stick it to the inside of a clear plastic bag. Then stick the bag to a page in your book with sticky tape.

But remember that many species have now become very rare because they have so often been picked.

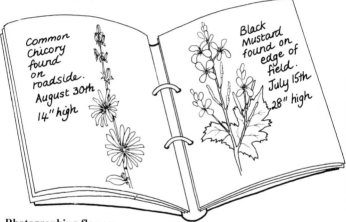

Photographing flowers

Photographs also make a good record of the flowers you find. Here are some tips to help you to take successful photographs.

Use a color film (slides are cheaper). Always take photographs with the sun behind you and make sure that your shadow does not fall on the flower. Try to photograph the whole plant so that the stem and leaves are visible.

With a simple camera, you cannot photograph flowers in close-up. A tall plant with large flowers or a patch of creeping plants will make good photographs.

If you lie flat on the ground and photograph a flower from below, outlined against the sky, it will stand out clearly; or you can prop a piece of black or colored cardboard up behind a flower to separate it from grass and leaves in the background.

Conservation of wild flowers

There are thousands of different kinds of wild flowers in America but this great variety, like plant life in many other parts of the world, is being threatened by various human actions.

Plants have been over-picked

In many areas, especially near big cities, some kinds of flowers have so often been picked by people (for bouquets or for study) that they have become rare.

It is now against the law to pick wild flowers in all national parks and in some state parks and forests. Certain flowers are also protected by law wherever they grow: it is illegal to pick California Poppies anywhere in California; and in New York state many plants, such as Trailing Arbutus, Harebell and Lady's-slipper, are also protected by law.

You can learn more about a flower from seeing it growing in the wild than by taking it home. So never pick a flower unless you are sure that you have identified it correctly and found that it is very common and not protected by law.

Habitats are being destroyed

A wild flower will reseed itself if its habitat (the sort of place where it lives) is not disturbed. But many habitats are being disturbed and destroyed by the spread of human civilization: cities and suburbs are expanding into fields and woodlands; marshes and swamps are being drained; and even the desert is being invaded by people looking for cheap land.

Habitats are being polluted

Fumes and gases from factories and cars pollute the air, making it hard for plants to breathe; they may also harm the insects needed for pollination. Pollution of soil and water is also harmful to plants.

What you can do

- If you are walking in a park, keep on the paths. Don't trample the flowers, and don't pick them.
- If you see other people picking wild flowers, explain why they shouldn't do this – because many are endangered, and once they have all been picked it will be too late to protect them.
- Join a conservation society (see page 57).

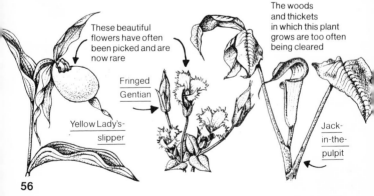

These beautiful flowers have often been picked and are now rare

Fringed Gentian

Yellow Lady's-slipper

The woods and thickets in which this plant grows are too often being cleared

Jack-in-the-pulpit

Books to read

Flowers. Herbert Zim and Alexander Martin (Golden Press). An inexpensive paperback. Color plates; flowers are arranged by color with range maps.

Newcomb's Wildflower Guide. Lawrence Newcomb (Little, Brown Co.). Covers northeast and north-central America. Flowers are arranged by key (explained). Color plates and black-and-white drawings. A good field guide.

A Field Guide to Wildflowers. Roger Tory Peterson and Margaret McKenny (Houghton, Mifflin Co.). Covers northeast and north-central North America. Flowers are arranged by color. Color plates and black-and-white drawings. A good field guide. Paperback, in the Peterson Field Guide series.

A Field Guide to Pacific States Wildflowers. Theodore F. Niehaus and Charles L. Ripper (Houghton, Mifflin Co.). Covers Washington, Oregon, California and near by areas. Hardcover, also in the Peterson Field Guide series, arranged and illustrated as above.

Wildflowers of Eastern America. John Klimas and James Cunningham (Knopf). A good identification book, has 304 color photos, but too big to put in your pocket. Flowers are arranged by color.

Wildflowers of Western America. Robert and Margaret Orr. Companion volume, same as above.

The Audubon Society Book of Wildflowers. Les Line and Walter Hodge (Abrams). A large, expensive book with nearly 200 color photos and an informative text.

Wildflowers of the United States. Harold Rickett (New York Botanical Garden). The most comprehensive book about wildflowers in the US. There are 6 volumes, one for each major region. Flowers are arranged by family. There are color photos and black-and-white drawings. This reference work can be found in some large public libraries.

Organizations you can join

A few of the nationwide conservation organizations are listed below. Most states also have conservation organizations, as do many communities.

American Museum of Natural History, Central Park West at 79 Street, New York, NY 10024.

Friends of the Earth, 124 Spear Street, San Francisco, CA 94105.

National Wildlife Federation, 1412 16 Street NW, Washington, DC 20036.

The Nature Conservancy, 1800 N. Kent Street, Arlington, VA 22209.

New England Wildflower Society, Inc., Hemenway Road, Framingham, MA 01701.

Sierra Club, 530 Bush Street, San Francisco, CA 94108.

The Wilderness Society, 1901 Pennsylvania Avenue NW, Washington, DC 20006.

Montreal Botanical Gardens, 4101 Sherbrooke Street, Montreal.

*Have local chapters.

Scorecard

When you have seen and identified a wild flower, use this scorecard to look up the number of points you have scored.

The flowers are arranged here in alphabetical order. Before looking up your score, look at the map below to find out which area you have found the plant in. You will find that the map of North America has been divided into six different areas, each of which show separate scores.

A low score (the lowest is 5) means that the flower is common and quite easy to find; the highest score is 25, and the higher the score, the rarer or more interesting the flower.

Some flowers, like Wild Carrot, are common throughout North America and therefore have a score of 5 for each area. Others, like Wood-betony, are fairly common in some areas and rare in others.

If no score is shown, this means that the flower does not grow in that area.

When you have found your score, you can either mark it in pencil in the book, or you can keep a record of your score in a notebook, making a note of the date and place where you spot the flower. Either way you can add up your total score whenever you like – at the end of each day, week or month.

Species (Name of flower)	1	2	3	4	5	6	Species (Name of flower)	1	2	3	4	5	6
Adder's-tongue, Coast					15		Buckwheat, Wild				15	15	15
Adder's-tongue, Yellow	5	15					Bugler, Scarlet				10		
Anemone	10			20	20	10	Bunchberry	15			15	10	15
Arbutus, Trailing	15	15					Buttercup, Swamp	10					20
Arrowhead	10	10	10	10	10	10	Butterfly-weed	10	10	10	15		10
Aster, New England	15	20		20	15	10	Cancer-root, One-flowered	15	15	15	15	15	15
Baby Blue-eyes					15	15	Cardinal-flower	20	20	20	20		20
Baneberry, Red	15			15	15	15	Carrot, Wild	5	5	5	5	5	5
Beardtongue	10	10	10			15	Chia				10	15	20
Bear-grass					10	10	Chicory, Common	5	5	10	5	5	5
Bee-plant, Rocky Mountain	15		20	10	10	10	Chickweed, Common	5	5	5	5	5	5
Bergamot, Wild	10	10	15				Chinese Houses				10	10	
Bindweed, Field	5	5	5	5	5	5	Clarkia, Tongue				15	15	15
Bitter Root				20	20	20	Clover, Red	5	5	5	5	5	5
Black-eyed Susan	5	5	5	10	5	5	Clover, White Sweet	5	5	5	5	5	5
Bladderwort, Greater	20	20	20	20	25	20	Columbine, Blue				20		15
Blanket-flower	15	15	10	10		10	Columbine, Wild	15	20	15			15
Blazing-star, Purple	15	20	15	20		15	Coralroot, Spotted	25	25	25	25	25	25
Blazing-star, Yellow				15	15	15	Cranesbill, Wild	10	10				20
Bleeding-heart, Western					15		Daisy, Ox-eye	5	5	10	5	5	5
Bloodroot	10	10	20			15	Dandelion, Common	5	5	5	5	5	5
Bluets	10	10					Dayflower, Asiatic	5	5	10			15
Bluebells	15	15				25	Dogbane, Spreading	5	5	10	10	5	5
Bouncing Bet	5	5	5	10	5	5	Dutchman's-breeches	10	15			20	15
Brooklime, American	10	15	10	10	10	10	Evening Primrose, Common	5	5	10		10	10

Species (Name of flower)	Scores for each area						Species (Name of flower)	Scores for each area					
	1	2	3	4	5	6		1	2	3	4	5	6
Evening Primrose, Tufted			25	15	20	15	Ipomopsis			15	15	15	15
Fiddleneck			15	10	10	15	Ironweed	10	10	25			20
Fireweed	10	20		10	10	10	Jack-in-the-pulpit	10	10	15			20
Flag, Blue	10						Jimsonweed	5	5	5	5		5
Flax, Prairie	10		10	10	10	10	Lady's-slipper, Yellow	20	20	20	25	20	20
Fleabane, Common	10	10	10	10	10	10	Lady's-thumb	5	5	5	5	5	5
Frostweed	10	25				15	Larkspur	10		15			15
Gentian, Fringed	20	25					Lily, Checker-				20	20	25
Gilia				15		25	Lily, Common Orange Day-	5	5	10			
Ginger, Wild	10	25				25	Lily, Fragrant Water-	10	10	10	10		20
Goldenrod	10	10	10		15	10	Lily, Leopard				25	20	
Gourd, Buffalo-	15		10	10	15	10	Lily, Sego-				20	20	15
Grass, Blue-eyed	5	5	15			20	Lily, Wood	20	20	20	20	20	20
Grass-of-Parnassus	15					25	Linanthus				10	20	25
Gumweed				5	5	10	Loosestrife, Purple	10	10				15
Harebell	15		15	15	15	15	Lupine				10		20
Heal-all	5	5	5	5	5	5	May-apple	10	10	15			25
Heliotrope, Seaside	15	5	5	5	5	5	Meadow-beauty, Virginia	15	10	10			20
Heliotrope, Wild				5	10	15	Milkwort, Yellow	20	15				
Hellebore, False				10	10	10	Miner's Lettuce				5	5	5
Hepatica, Round-lobed	10	10					Monkey-flower	10	10	25			10
Hyacinth, Water	25	5	5	25			Monkey-flower, Common	5			5	5	10
Indian-pipe	15	15	15		15	15	Monument Plant			15	15	15	15
Indian Warrior				15	15		Morning-glory, Common	5	5	5	5	5	5
Indigo, White False	10	10	20			20	Moss, Spanish	25	10	10			

Species (Name of flower)	1	2	3	4	5	6	Species (Name of flower)	1	2	3	4	5	6
Mullein, Common	5	5	5	5	5	5	Rose-pink	15	10	15			20
Mustard, Black	5	5	10	5	5	5	Rose, Swamp-	10	15				
Nettle, Horse-	5	5	5	5	5	5	Rue, Early Meadow-	10	15				20
Onion, Nodding	10	10	20	25	15	10	Ruellia, Hairy	15	10	15			
Orchis, Smaller Purple-fringed	20	25					St Johnswort, Common	5	5	5	10	5	5
Orchis, Stream			20	20	15	20	Shinleaf	20			20	25	20
Paint-brush, Scarlet				10	10	10	Shooting-star				15	15	
Parsnip, Cow	10	10		10	10	10	Silverweed	10			15	15	10
Partridgeberry	10	10	15				Skunk Cabbage	10	20				20
Pasque-flower	20		25	20	20	15	Snapdragon				10		
Pea, Partridge-	10	5	5	15		15	Soapweed	25	25	15	20		10
Petunia, Seaside	15	10	10	15	15		Solomon's-seal, False	5	5	5	5	5	5
Phlox, Blue	10	15	20			20	Sorrel, Creeping Lady's-	5	5	10	5	5	5
Pink, Deptford	5	10			10	10	Spiderwort	5	5	10			15
Pipsissewa	10	15		10	10	15	Spring-beauty	5	10	10			
Pokeweed	10	10	10				Spurge, Flowering	10	10	10			15
Poppy, California		10		15	10	10	Strawberry	5	10	10		10	10
Poppy, Prickly			10	20		10	Sunflower, Common	5	5	5	5	5	5
Prickly Pear, Eastern	15	10	10			15	Teasel, Wild	10	15			10	10
Pride of California				20			Thistle, Bull	5	5		5	5	5
Primrose, Parry's				25		20	Thoroughwort	5	5	10			10
Puccoon, Hoary	15	15				15	Tickseed	15	10	15	10	10	15
Puncture Vine	10	5	5	5	5	5	Toadflax, Old-field	10	10	10	10	10	10
Pussy Paws				10	10	20	Touch-me-not, Spotted	10	10			15	15
Red Maids				5	5		Trillium, White	10	15				

Species (Name of flower)	Scores for each area						Species (Name of flower)	Scores for each area					
	1	2	3	4	5	6		1	2	3	4	5	6
Unicorn-plant	15	15	15	20	15	20	Violet, Downy Yellow	10	20				20
Venus' Looking-glass	10	10	10	15	10	10	Violet, Western Dog	20			15	10	15
Verbena, Yellow Sand-				10	10		Virgin's-bower	20			15	15	15
Vervain, Rose	15	10	10			15	Wallflower, Western	15	20	10	5	5	5
Vetch, Hairy	5	5	10	10	5	5	Wood-betony	10	10	10	15		25
Vetch, Milk-				15	15	20	Yarrow, Common	5	5	5	5	5	5
Violet, Birdfoot	10	10	15			15	Yerba Mansa			15	10	15	20

Index

The common name of each flower is listed here with the page number(s) beside it. The Latin name, which you will need to know for further study, appears below in *italics*. If a flower has another common name which is also widely used, this is shown in parentheses after the first common name.